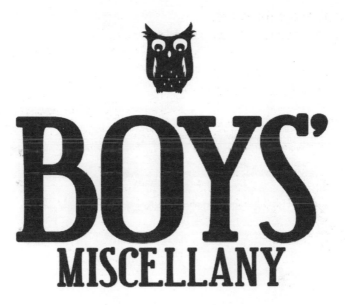

BOYS'
MISCELLANY

Fascinating information
every boy should know

Written by Martin Oliver

Illustrated by Mike Phillips

Cover illustrations by Agnese Baruzzi
Edited by Bryony Jones
Designed by Barbara Ward
Cover designed by Angie Allison

BOYS'
MISCELLANY

Sandy Creek
NEW YORK

An Imprint of Sterling Publishing
387 Park Avenue South
New York, NY 10016

This 2013 edition published by Sandy Creek.
First published in Great Britain in 2012 by Buster Books,
an imprint of Michael O'Mara Books Limited.

The image on page 68 is by Andrew Pinder
The image on page 112 is by Martin Remphry

ISBN 978-1-4351-5047-8

Manufactured by CPI Group (UK) Ltd, Croydon,
CR0 4YY, United Kingdom.

Lot #:
2 4 6 8 10 9 7 5 3 1
07/13

Contents

Extreme Hobbies

Super Stilts
Run faster, jump higher, and push yourself to the limit with stilts on springs.

Zorbing
Strap yourself into a giant ball and roll down a steep slope. Away you goooooo!

Sky Diving
Throwing yourself out of a plane never gets boring, no matter how often you do it.

Underwater Hockey
It's just like normal hockey, but it's played under water and no oxygen tanks are allowed.

Cave Diving
Combine the thrill of caving with the skill of diving, navigating through flooded underground cave systems.

Heli-Skiing
Jump out of a helicopter on to a high mountain slope and ski through untouched snow. Watch out for avalanches.

Shark-Cage Diving
Come face to face with a great white shark. Not for the faint-hearted!

Extreme Ironing
Make ironing more exciting by doing it at the top of a mountain or under water.

Parkour
Make journeys more interesting – explore the world by jumping, rolling, and running around obstacles.

Useful Space Spin-Offs

You don't have to be an astronaut to enjoy some of the
benefits of space travel. Here are some products invented by
NASA for space exploration that have come in handy on Earth.

Invisible Braces
You too can have a
Hollywood smile without tell-tale
"train tracks," because invisible braces
contain a material called TPA, invented by NASA
to protect the antennae on spacecraft.

Too-Cool-For-School Sneakers
Shoe companies have taken inspiration from space boots,
using insoles that reduce impact and improve ventilation
— so no aching ankles or smelly feet for you!

Super-Fast Swimsuit
There's no water on the Moon, but the principles that
help stop spaceships being slowed down as they
travel through air have been used to develop
super-fast swimsuits that reduce friction
so that swimmers can speed
through the water.

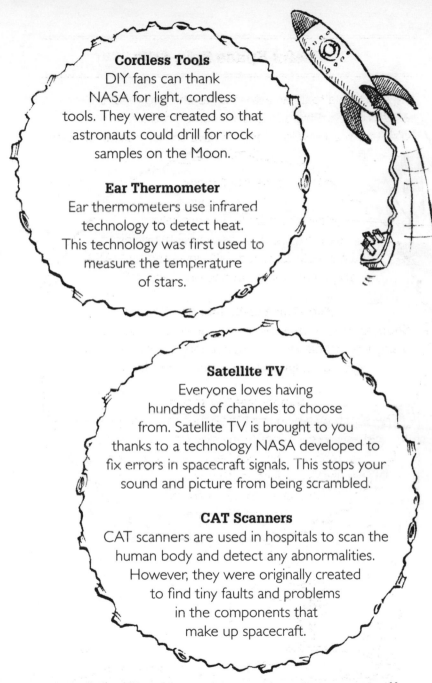

Cordless Tools

DIY fans can thank NASA for light, cordless tools. They were created so that astronauts could drill for rock samples on the Moon.

Ear Thermometer

Ear thermometers use infrared technology to detect heat. This technology was first used to measure the temperature of stars.

Satellite TV

Everyone loves having hundreds of channels to choose from. Satellite TV is brought to you thanks to a technology NASA developed to fix errors in spacecraft signals. This stops your sound and picture from being scrambled.

CAT Scanners

CAT scanners are used in hospitals to scan the human body and detect any abnormalities. However, they were originally created to find tiny faults and problems in the components that make up spacecraft.

Egyptian Explorers In America?

In 1990, during a dig in the desert near Guadalupe, USA, archaeologists made a series of incredible discoveries. Underneath the sandy dunes, they found what appeared to be the remains of a giant statue of a pharaoh, items of clothing, and harnesses for chariots. Were they about to turn history on its head and prove that ancient Egyptian explorers had reached America?

Er, no. The remains they had found were built as part of the set of a 1923 epic movie, *The Ten Commandments*. The set was one of the largest ever built and included huge statues, temples, and buildings up to ten stories high.

When the cameras stopped rolling, the set was huge and would cost too much money to move, so a large trench was dug in the desert and everything was bulldozed into it.

Buzzing Bees

- There can be more than 60,000 bees in a bee colony. Life must get pretty crowded.

- Honey bees flap their wings an amazing 11,000 times a minute. This causes the buzzing sound you can hear when they fly.

- Bees visit more than two million flowers and fly 90,000km (56,000 miles) to make one 500g (17.6oz) jar of honey.

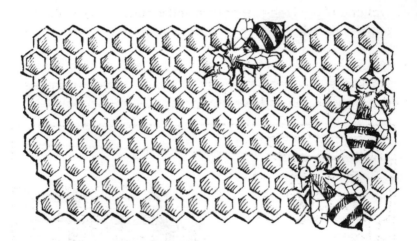

- An average worker bee will only make $\frac{1}{12}$ of a teaspoon of honey in its lifetime – that's not enough to cover a single piece of toast!

- If a bee ate two tablespoons of honey, it would have enough energy to fly around the world.

Titanic Failures

The *Titanic* was a huge ship that sank in 1912 – but do you know the fates of the two other ships in the fleet, the *Olympic* and the *Britannic?*

The *Olympic*
Launched in 1911, the *Olympic* had an unfortunate habit of crashing into other ships. On her fifth voyage, she collided with a warship and was out of action for three months. In 1934 the *Olympic* had another collision. This one was off the American coast. The boat she hit sank completely, and a year later the *Olympic* was retired and scrapped, which was probably for the best!

The *Britannic*
The *Britannic* was launched in 1914. To stop history repeating itself she was given extra lifeboats and more safety features than the *Titanic*. But in 1916 she was sunk during the First World War, and despite her safety features, she actually sank in under an hour. Luckily, over a thousand of her passengers were rescued and only 30 souls were lost at sea.

Pesky Parasites

A "parasite" is a plant or animal that lives on or in another living thing. Here are some disgusting parasites that just love humans.

Tapeworms
Tapeworms can live inside your gut, and can grow to a huge 9m (30ft) long – all curled up in your intestines. They can live there so quietly you might not even know you've got one.

Human Botfly
Human botflies are large, hairy flies that lay eggs on your skin. The eggs hatch into larvae, which dig through the skin and live inside your body, feeding on your blood. When they're ready, they dig their way back out.

Bedbugs
Bedbugs live in and near beds – which gives them their name. They wait until you're fast asleep, then pop out for a good feed on your blood. You'll wake up with itchy little bumps where they've munched.

YUM!

Leeches
Leeches are worms with suckers at one end and a taste for human blood. Their spit has a special ingredient to stop your blood from clotting, so that they can suck for longer.

The Best Things Come In Threes

- The letter W the start of every web address
- Places on the winners' podium
- Number of scores to make a hat-trick
- Bones in a human ear
- Wise men in the Nativity
- Billy Goats Gruff
- Starting instructions for a race
- Harry, Hermione, and Ron
- Strikes before you're out
- Wise monkeys
- Bears
- Musketeers.

Why Do Tightrope Walkers Carry A Long Pole?

The reason tightrope walkers carry poles is all to do with something called "inertia." Carrying a pole – the longer the better – spreads the walker's mass out over a larger area. If someone's mass is spread out, they are said to have "high inertia," and this means that they move slowly. Any wobbles or false moves take place much more slowly, so the walker is able to correct them – and not fall off the rope.

Make 'Em Laugh

There are many different ways to laugh. Here are just a few.

The Titter
A polite, restrained laugh that shows appreciation, but not outright laughter.

The Snicker
When you're laughing at something you really shouldn't find funny.

The Donkey
A repetitive hee-haw sound.

The Giggle
This usually happens when you are a bit embarrassed or nervous, but feel you should laugh out of politeness.

The Gasp
When you're laughing so much you can hardly breathe.

The Splutter
An explosive laugh that occurs when a hilarious event takes you by surprise.

The Guffaw
The loudest laugh of all, reserved only for the funniest moments.

The Hollow Laugh
A weak, humorless laugh that you usually perform to join in with others.

The Earth is hit by around 100 lightning bolts every second.

The air around a lightning bolt gets so hot that it can reach five times the temperature of the surface of the Sun.

Lightning kills around 2,000 people each year.

Rubber shoes won't protect you from lightning.

You can be struck by lightning from a storm 16km (10 miles) away – even if the sky above you is blue.

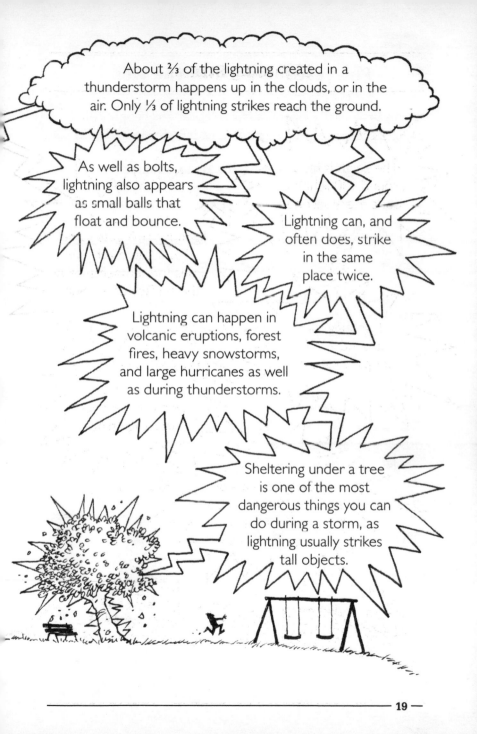

About ⅔ of the lightning created in a thunderstorm happens up in the clouds, or in the air. Only ⅓ of lightning strikes reach the ground.

As well as bolts, lightning also appears as small balls that float and bounce.

Lightning can, and often does, strike in the same place twice.

Lightning can happen in volcanic eruptions, forest fires, heavy snowstorms, and large hurricanes as well as during thunderstorms.

Sheltering under a tree is one of the most dangerous things you can do during a storm, as lightning usually strikes tall objects.

Fun Festivals Around The World

Each year, weird and wonderful celebrations happen all around the globe. Here are some of the strangest.

Day Of The Dead, Mexico
This festival features beautiful yet spooky skeletons, skulls, and other symbols of death. But it's actually a happy and colorful celebration rather than a sad event.

Monkey Buffet, Thailand
The town of Lopburi attracts many tourists, who come to see its monkeys. Every year the town throws the monkeys a party to thank them for bringing it wealth. Chefs prepare sausages, fruit, jelly, and ice cream for the 2,000 monkeys.

El Colacho, Spain
Also known as The Devil's Jump, this festival involves dressing up as the devil and leaping over newborn babies. It celebrates the Christian festival of Corpus Christi, and it's meant to prevent illness and put off evil spirits — just as long as the person jumping doesn't slip up.

Boryeong Mud Festival, South Korea
There's only one way to enjoy this festival — by taking the plunge. Designed to celebrate the healing power of mud, the festival involve visitors playing around in the squelchy stuff.

Putting You Right About Pirates

No one is absolutely sure how the name "Jolly Roger" for pirate flags came about. Some people think it was named after the devil, who is sometimes called "Old Roger." Others believe it came from the French words "jolie rouge," which were used to name a red flag that was used in naval warfare, and by early pirates.

There is no reliable evidence that pirates ever made their victims walk the plank. In fact, it's unlikely that they ever did – why bother, when you could just kill them quickly, or throw them into the sea from the side of the boat?

In the 17th century there were so many pirates in the Caribbean that they set up their own city. Port Royal in Jamaica became a base for thousands of pirates. The city was known as "the wickedest and richest city in the world." Its reign of terror didn't last too long, however, as a massive earthquake struck in 1692, killing thousands of people and washing the city into the sea.

Military Formations Used By The Roman Army

The Phalanx

The *phalanx* was first used by the ancient Greeks, then by the early Roman army as their basic formation. Armed soldiers lined up in rows. The soldiers in the first few rows held out their spears (*hastae*) horizontally in front of them, to stab enemies when they charged. At the same time, they held up their shields to make a solid wall to protect themselves. The soldiers in the rows behind them held their spears up vertically, so they didn't accidentally stab anyone in front. Ouch!

The Tortoise

If the Roman army was attacked by arrows or objects dropped from above, the soldiers would hold their shields over their heads, while the soldiers around the edge of the group would hold their shields upright to form a barrier.

No prizes for guessing why it was called "the tortoise."

The Wedge

This formation was used when the army was on the attack. It was designed so that soldiers could use their short swords (*gladii*). They stood in a triangle, with one soldier at the tip, and thrust forward into enemy lines. The aim of the wedge was to split enemy soldiers into smaller groups and to restrict their movements so they could not fight back very effectively.

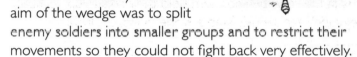

The Orb

If a group of soldiers became separated from the ranks and were surrounded by the enemy, or if the Romans were losing a battle and had split up into small groups, they formed into orbs. They stood in a circle with their shields on the outside, so they could keep fighting until reinforcements could arrive to help them. Officers would stand in the center of the orb, so that they were protected.

How To Do A Perfect Sprint Start

1. Lower yourself into the blocks and crouch with your back knee on the ground. Place your hands just behind the starting line, and form a high arch between your fingers and thumbs.

2. When the race is ready to start, shift your balance forward so that your weight is on your fingertips. Breathe slowly and try to relax.

3. The starter will say, "Ready, set, go!" When you hear the word "set," lift up your hips so they're higher than your shoulders.

Lean your body as far forward as possible. Keep your head at a comfortable angle. Don't try to look up at the track. Breathe in, and be ready for the starting signal.

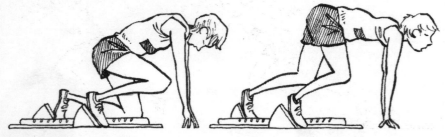

Bruise Biology

A bruise is caused when blood leaks from blood vessels under the skin. At first a bruise is reddish, because the blood that you can see through the skin is fresh. After one or two days, the bruise turns purplish blue, as the blood starts to break down. After around a week, it will turn green, then yellow and brown as something called "bile pigment" is made. It eventually fades, as the blood is absorbed back into the body.

4. As soon as you hear the "g" of "go," push yourself out of the blocks. Don't go too early, or you will false start.

Breathe out hard and pump your arms and legs, but don't fall over! Keep your body low and your eyes on the ground as you explode out of the blocks.

5. As you start to speed up, gradually raise your body to its full height. Thrust your elbows as high as possible with each backward swing, and lift up your knees.

6. By the time you've run a third of the distance, you should be upright and into your full sprinting stride. Run as fast as you can toward the finish line.

Newborn Names

Some animal babies have the strangest names.

- A gorilla has an infant
- A hare has a leveret
- A shark has a pup
- A crocodile has a hatchling
- A skunk has a kit

- A trout has a fly or a fingerling
- A pigeon has a squab
- A platypus has a puggle
- A turkey has a poult.

Love playing practical jokes? Then here's a round-up of some of the most famous tricks and hoaxes from history.

The Trojan Horse
According to legend, the ten-year-long Trojan War between the Greeks and the Trojans ended when the Greeks fooled the Trojans into thinking that they had given up and gone home. They left behind a large wooden horse as an offering.

The unsuspecting Trojans dragged the horse into their city, not realizing that it was crammed full of Greek soldiers, who crept out in the dead of night, opened the city gates to let their fellow soldiers in, and captured the city.

Piltdown Man
Scientists were amazed in 1912 when they were shown fossilized remains of what looked like a skull from an early human. The remains appeared to be the proof of a link between apes and early man. The bones set off years of debate among scientists, because they were so different

from other remains of early man that had already been discovered. In fact, they were too good to be true – after 40 years of confusion, the remains turned out to be fake. Instead of being an example of ancient man, someone had mixed human, orangutan, and chimpanzee remains.

Mermen And Mermaids

People in the 17th and 18th centuries were amazed when visitors to East Asia returned with what seemed to be mummified remains of mermen and mermaids. They became known as "monkey fish" and were displayed in circuses to amaze crowds. However, recent investigations have revealed that the creatures had been made from the head of a monkey, sewn to a fish tail, and filled with papier-mâché.

The War Of The Worlds

Imagine turning on the radio and discovering that the world is in the middle of a Martian invasion. That's exactly what happened in America in 1938, when a radio play of a book called *The War of the Worlds* by H. G. Wells was broadcast. It was so realistic that millions of people thought an invasion was actually happening and began fleeing their homes.

Naming A Force Of Nature

What links the names Valerie, Oscar, Florence, and Gordon? No, they're not long-lost cousins, they're hurricane names.

Every hurricane is given a name, chosen from a list by the World Meteorological Organization (WMO). Once each storm is given a name, it is easier to identify and track.

Each name on the list begins with a different letter of the alphabet – for example, Alberto, Beryl, and Chris. Every letter is used apart from Q, U, X, Y, and Z.

In 1953, hurricanes were given female names, just like ships are.

Men's names were added to the list in 1979.

Originally, hurricanes were identified by geographical location. This was rather confusing, as hurricanes don't stay still!

If a storm causes lots of damage, as Hurricane Irene did in America in 2011, its name is wiped off the list and never used again. Over 40 names have been dropped since 1954, including Floyd, Igor, and Luis.

I'VE NEVER LIKED THE NAME FLOYD!

Crazy Competitions

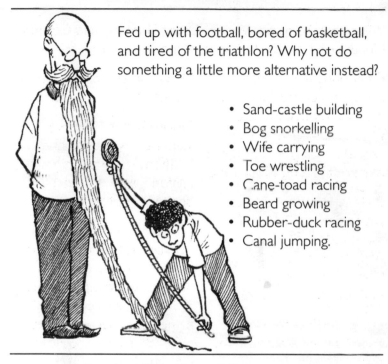

Fed up with football, bored of basketball, and tired of the triathlon? Why not do something a little more alternative instead?

- Sand-castle building
- Bog snorkelling
- Wife carrying
- Toe wrestling
- Cane-toad racing
- Beard growing
- Rubber-duck racing
- Canal jumping.

Sports Stadium Nicknames

Sports grounds are often given nicknames by the supporters of the teams that play there. Here are some of the best.

- The Chocolate Box (Boca Juniors Stadium, Argentina)
- House Of Pain (Carisbrook Stadium, New Zealand)
- The Lady In Black (Darlington Raceway, USA)
- The Big Egg (Tokyo Dome, Japan)
- The Graveyard (Olympic Park, Australia)
- Theatre Of Dreams (Old Trafford Stadium, UK)
- The Dinghy (Allianz Arena, Munich, Germany).

The Nobel Prize

The Nobel Prize is one of the most famous awards in the world, but what do you actually know about it?

The Nobel Prize was first awarded in 1901. Winners receive a medal, a certificate, and some lovely cash.

The scheme was founded by a rich Swede, Alfred Nobel. After he died in 1896, he left money in his will, to be given to people each year who have done the most for mankind.

Prizes are given to people who have done great work in Physics, Literature, Peace, Chemistry, Physiology, and Medicine. In 1968, a new category, Economic Sciences, was added.

Nobel Prizes are not awarded every year – if nothing comes up to scratch during a year, then no prizes are given out.

He created an award for peace, but much of Alfred Nobel's wealth actually came from his invention of dynamite and ownership of a company that made weapons.

The oldest Nobel Prize winner was Leonid Hurwicz. He was 90 years old when he received the prize for Economic Sciences in 2007.

The youngest Nobel Prize winner so far was Lawrence Bragg – who was just 25 years old when he won the Physics prize in 1915.

Famous winners include Theodore Roosevelt (1906), Martin Luther King Jr (1964), Mother Teresa (1979), Nelson Mandela (1993), and the Burmese politician Aung San Suu Kyi (1991).

Tasty Types Of Pasta

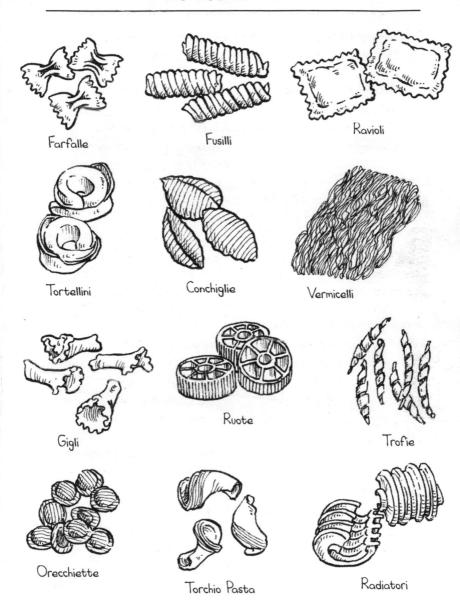

Farfalle

Fusilli

Ravioli

Tortellini

Conchiglie

Vermicelli

Gigli

Ruote

Trofie

Orecchiette

Torchio Pasta

Radiatori

Great Escapes

Escape From Alcatraz

Alcatraz prison, in the San Francisco Bay, was built on an island surrounded by very cold water, with strong currents that would sweep swimmers away. This was the perfect way to keep prisoners imprisoned.

THE WATER LOOKS A BIT CHILLY TO ME, I THINK I'LL STAY IN MY CELL!

However, it is possible that one escape attempt may have succeeded. In 1962, three prisoners escaped outside the prison walls and were never seen again – no one knows if they made it to freedom, or met a watery end.

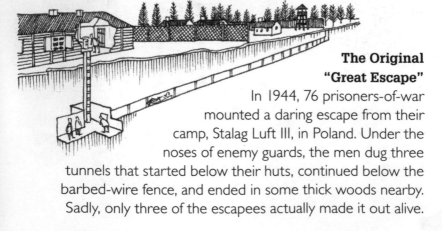

The Original "Great Escape"

In 1944, 76 prisoners-of-war mounted a daring escape from their camp, Stalag Luft III, in Poland. Under the noses of enemy guards, the men dug three tunnels that started below their huts, continued below the barbed-wire fence, and ended in some thick woods nearby. Sadly, only three of the escapees actually made it out alive.

Chilean Miners

Perhaps the most remarkable escape ever made was by 33 miners in Chile. In 2010, they were trapped in a mine after a huge landslide. For over two weeks, people thought that the men had all been killed. Then, against all odds, they were found alive.

Rescuers worked around the clock to drill a rescue shaft through the rock. In the meantime, food and drink were passed to the miners through a narrow hole. Finally, the miners were lifted back to the surface, one by one, after two months below ground.

NOT CHEESE SANDWICHES AGAIN!

A Mummy Zoo

Archaeologists have discovered mummified ...

... dogs
... bulls
... hawks

... gazelles
... crocodiles
... lizards

... fish
... beetles
... cats.

Extreme Sporting Challenges

Some people love to test themselves in truly tough sporting challenges. Here are some of the most grueling.

Raid World Championship
This team race lasts at least five days and competitors cover a distance of about 200km (124 miles). They might test their skills at mountain biking, climbing, skiing, kayaking, or inline skating, but the sports involved change every year.

La Ruta De Los Conquistadores
This three-day event in Costa Rica is the ultimate in mountain-biking endurance. Crazy competitors have to pedal through dense jungle and clinging mud, cross rivers and scale mountains in tropical heat and freezing cold temperatures.

Iditarod Trail Sled Dog Race
This race follows a historic supply route for Alaskan miners that is around 1,600km (1,000 miles) long. "Mushers" and their teams of sled dogs battle hostile conditions as they make their way across the freezing Arctic, through thick forests and over treacherous mountains.

Marathon Des Sables
This "ultramarathon" is for runners who don't find a normal 42km (26 mile) marathon long enough. Runners have to cover about 246km (150 miles) in six days in the hot Sahara Desert. To add to the fun, they have to carry all their food and kit with them.

The Frisbee

In the 1920s, college students played a throwing game, similar to Frisbee, using pie tins, which were made by the Frisbie Pie Company. Thirty years later, the plastic Frisbee, or "pluto platter," as it was known, was invented. The Frisbie nickname came back to life and became so popular that eventually the pluto platter was renamed the "Frisbee."

Great Places To ... Spot A Celebrity

Fancy spotting a celebrity? You might want to hang out in the following places.

- Telluride, USA (ski resort)
- Goldeneye Resort, Jamaica
- Gstaad, Switzerland (ski resort)
- Sveti Stefan, Montenegro (luxury hotel)
- South Beach, Miami, USA
- Ibiza, Balearic Islands
- St. Barts, Caribbean
- Côte d'Azur, France
- Wakaya, Fiji (holiday resort)
- The Hamptons, USA.

Blackbeard's Last Battle

When it came to piracy, Edward Teach – also known as Blackbeard – put other villains in the shade. He was a huge man with long hair and a flowing beard. He would go into battle armed with a fearsome cutlass and an array of pistols. To complete the effect, he would stick lit fuses in his hair.

In 1718, Lieutenant Maynard, of the British Navy, was given the job of getting rid of Blackbeard. This is what some say happened …

Blackbeard was shot, and slashed in the neck with a cutlass, but somehow stayed on his feet. Finally, after being surrounded by attackers, he slumped to the deck, dead. He had been shot five times and stabbed in 20 places.

Maynard cut off his opponent's head and pushed the body into the sea. Blackbeard's body swam seven times around the ship before slowly sinking below the waves.

Gross Smells

Got a sensitive nose? Then you'll want to avoid the following – they're particularly pungent.

Cheese – The Vieux Boulogne cheese's smell comes from being matured by washing it with beer – hmmm, lovely.

Fruit – The durian is a fruit that is meant to taste like vanilla, but stinks like blocked drains when it's opened.

Plant – Rafflesia, a plant that is charmingly known as the "corpse flower," apparently smells worse than a rotting buffalo.

Animal – The striped polecat is a kind of weasel whose cute appearance is misleading. It has glands that give off a stink so powerful that one striped polecat has been seen to make three hungry lions back away in disgust.

Place – Rotorua, New Zealand, has a rotten-eggy smell that comes from sulfur dioxide, released from steam vents and mud pools.

Fearsome Foods And Dangerous Delicacies

Some foods should carry health warnings. Check out this dangerous dining menu of foods from around the world.

MAIN COURSES

Namibian Bullfrog – It doesn't look very tasty, but this giant bullfrog is a delicacy in Namibia. Unfortunately, it contains poison strong enough to cause kidney failure and death. Vigorous cooking in a pot that has been lined with dry wood is believed to neutralize the poison, making it safe to eat.

Fugu – Fugu is a fish that contains enough poison to kill 30 people. It is prepared by Japanese fugu chefs who are trained for years to learn how to serve the fish without killing their customers.

Sannakji – This Korean delicacy is octopus with a twist – the octopus is still alive and wriggling. The octopus's tentacles need to be chewed thoroughly – there are reports of diners choking, as the suction cups attach themselves to the inside of their throats.

Hot Dogs – A recent study in the USA revealed that 17% of children's fatal food accidents are caused by choking on hot dogs.

SIDE DISHES

Ackee – This is a fruit that goes perfectly with saltfish in Jamaica's national dish. But don't be impatient – if you open the fruit before it's ripe, or eat its black seeds, you'll be in for a dose of vomiting, which can result in a coma or even death.

Red Kidney Beans – These are delicious when boiled properly and cooked with chilli, but they can be lethal if eaten raw. They contain a toxic substance called lectin that can cause vomiting and death.

Green Salad And Vegetables – Eat your greens, but only if you've washed them. The vomiting bug, Norovirus, along with E. coli, can sometimes be spread by people eating salads or green vegetables that have not been cleaned properly.

DANGEROUS DESSERTS

Cassava – If prepared wrongly, the cassava plant can actually produce a deadly poison called cyanide.

Star Fruit – If you have damaged or delicate kidneys, it's best to avoid star fruit. Even a small amount could affect your nervous system and brain, and give you seizures.

Casu Marzu – This sheep's cheese contains a special ingredient – live maggots. It's always a good idea to brush them off before taking a big bite as the maggots can, on very rare occasions, survive inside your stomach and cause bleeding, vomiting, and diarrhea, as they try to break out of your stomach wall.

Famous Firsts

1. The first US president was George Washington.

1. The first people to climb Mount Everest were Edmund Hillary and Tenzing Norgay.

1. The first man in space was Yuri Gagarin.

1. The first dog in space was called Laika.

1. The first ever billionaire was John D. Rockefeller.

1. The first cloned mammal was Dolly the sheep.

1. The first Roman emperor was Augustus Caesar.

1. The first US state was Delaware.

1. The first solo flight across the Atlantic was by Charles Lindbergh.

1. The first Bond film was *Dr. No.*

1. The first satellite to orbit the Earth was Sputnik I.

1. The first woman, according to Greek myth, was Pandora.

1. The first person to run a mile in under four minutes was Roger Bannister.

1. The first 1080° on a skateboard – three-and-a-half full rotations in mid air – was performed by Tom Schaar, aged 12.

The Human Brain

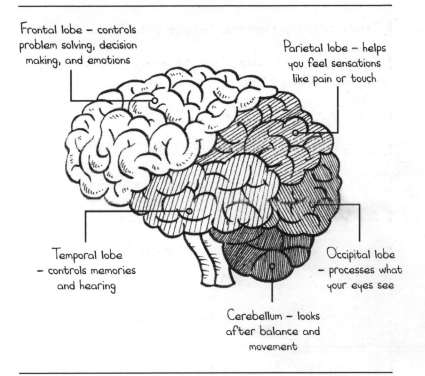

Frontal lobe – controls problem solving, decision making, and emotions

Parietal lobe – helps you feel sensations like pain or touch

Temporal lobe – controls memories and hearing

Occipital lobe – processes what your eyes see

Cerebellum – looks after balance and movement

Animal Brain Bonanza

A giraffe's brain is 16 times lighter than its heart.

The giant squid's brain is doughnut-shaped. When it eats, it has to chew food into small pieces so that the food can fit down its throat, which is surrounded by the ring-shaped brain.

A woodpecker's brain is surrounded by a bone that acts like a seatbelt to protect it when it taps at wood with its beak.

Jolly Rogers

Seeing a Jolly Roger flag fluttering from the mast of a pirate ship would strike fear into the hearts of sailors. Different pirates had their own flags, which they would raise as a way of frightening merchant ships into surrendering. These are the flags of some of the most fearsome pirates ever seen on the high seas.

Blackbeard was one of the most ferocious pirates of all time, and his flag was designed to shiver more than the odd timber. It showed a skeleton about to spear a human heart.

With a flag showing a muscled arm brandishing a sword called a scimitar, no one could mistake what would happen to them if Captain Tew and his crew had their way.

John Avery flew a flag decorated with a skull and crossbones. He captured a ship loaded with treasure, belonging to the ruler of India, but soon afterward Avery disappeared. No one knows what happened to him or the treasure.

Captain John Rackham was unusual among pirates because he allowed two female pirates, Anne Bonny and Mary Read, to fight as part of his crew. He liked to display a skull above two crossed swords on his flag.

Bartholomew Roberts was shown on his own flag, with a sword in his hand and a skull under each foot. ABH stands for "a Barbadian's head" and AMH stands for "a Martinican's head." You'd want to take care if you came from either of those countries!

Alien Invaders

Aliens invaders don't always have four eyes, green skin, or carry ray guns. Some plants and animals that have been taken to new parts of the world by humans have been far more destructive than any alien from outer space might be.

Cane Toads
Appearance: Big and ugly
Origin: Southern and
Central America
Now found: Australia

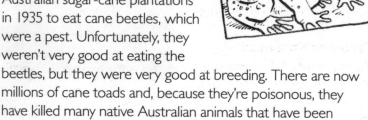

Cane toads were taken to
Australian sugar-cane plantations
in 1935 to eat cane beetles, which
were a pest. Unfortunately, they
weren't very good at eating the
beetles, but they were very good at breeding. There are now millions of cane toads and, because they're poisonous, they have killed many native Australian animals that have been foolish enough to eat them.

Zebra Mussels
Appearance: Small and stripy
Origin: The Black Sea
Now Found: Canadian lakes

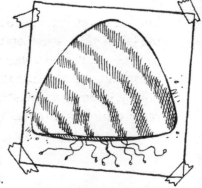

It's thought that zebra mussels
hitched a lift to Canada on a cargo
ship. They quickly bred and filled
the Canadian lakes, damaging ships
and blocking entrances to factories.

Burmese Pythons
Appearance: Big, long, and beautifully patterned
Origin: Southeast Asia
Now found: The Everglades, Florida, USA

Burmese pythons have settled into the swamps and forests of Florida. It's thought that the snakes, once owned by people as pets, have either been released by their owners, or have escaped from captivity. With few natural predators, the snakes have made themselves at home. They can live for up to 25 years, and grow to over 6m (20ft) in length. They've even been known to eat deer!

Japanese Knotweed
Appearance: A fast-growing plant that forms large clumps, 1–3m (3–10ft) high
Origin: Japan, Korea, and Taiwan
Now found: Europe and USA

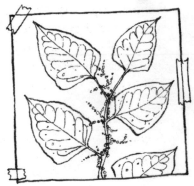

This plant was first introduced to the UK in 1825, and then taken to America. It grows very well in damp habitats, and spreads very quickly. It grows so densely that it strangles and kills lots of other plants that are native to Europe and the USA. Its large roots can destroy building foundations, roads, and paving.

Crazy Kings

Here are some of the more nutty rulers from history.

King Ludwig II Of Bavaria (1845–1886)
Ludwig became king while he was still a teenager. As he got older he hid away from the public and created his own fairy-tale life. He loved the opera and theater. It is rumored that he used to pretend to be characters from operas, and asked his courtiers to play along with him. He built beautiful, over-the-top, extravagant palaces to live in. Ludwig was eventually declared insane by a panel of doctors. A couple of days later, he was found mysteriously drowned in a lake.

Emperor Commodus (AD161–192)
Commodus was a Roman emperor who became more and more vicious after he survived a murder attempt. He renamed Rome "Colonia Commodiana," which means "the Colony of Commodus," and dressed up like the god Hercules.

He would attend gladiatorial games carrying a club and wearing a lion-skin, before shooting arrows at lions that were released in the arena. His reign ended when his advisers had him murdered. He was strangled by a champion wrestler.

Charles VI Of France (1368–1422)

Charles was known as "Charles the Mad." During one period of madness, Charles thought he was made of glass, and had iron rods put into his clothes to stop him from breaking.

Emperor Caligula (AD12–41)

Caligula is famous for being a really rotten ruler. A historian called Suetonius wrote that Caligula was bald on his head but very hairy everywhere else on his body, rather like a goat. Caligula made it a crime punishable by death to mention goats in his presence, or to look down on his bald head. He is also rumored to have built a special stable box for his favorite racehorse, invited it to dinner, and thought about promoting it to one of the most powerful positions within Rome – although no one knows if this is actually true.

George III Of England (1738–1820)

Historians think poor George had a disease called porphyria, which caused his insanity, but during his lifetime, doctors simply thought he was mad. He was very sensitive to light, and had dark reddish-purple urine. Over time, he had convulsions and lost his sight. During his fits, he was restrained and imprisoned in his private apartments.

Dynamic Sporting Debuts

Here are some men and women who have wowed the crowds with their first sporting appearances.

Eddy Merckx

Belgian cyclist Eddy Merckx was nicknamed "The Cannibal" for his appetite for winning. In 1969, on his first Tour de France – a famously difficult three-week-long bike race – he won all three prizes. He was given the yellow jersey for winning the race 18 minutes ahead of his rivals, the polka-dot jersey for being "King of the Mountains" (the best mountain climber) – and the green jersey for earning the most points over the race.

LeBron James

While he was still at school, LeBron James was compared to the basketball superstar Michael "Magic" Johnson. He soon lived up to his promise, and had a huge sponsorship deal from Nike before he even played a professional game of basketball. In his first season, playing for the Cleveland Cavaliers in 2003–4, he won more points, made more steals, and played for more minutes than anyone else on the team.

Boris Becker

In 1985, an unknown German teenager called Boris Becker won the Wimbledon tennis tournament. Aged 17, he was the youngest ever player to win.

Lionel Messi

Argentinian Lionel Messi is regarded as one of the best soccer players in history. He went to Spain, where he played for Barcelona, and in his first season he broke the record for the youngest player in the league, and the youngest soccer player to score a goal, when he was just 17 years, ten months, and seven days old. Unfortunately, Messi's career playing for his own country didn't have quite the same start. On his first match for Argentina, he was sent off after only 47 seconds.

Lewis Hamilton

Formula 1 racing driver Lewis Hamilton finished in third place in his first Grand Prix race in Melbourne, Australia, in 2007. He looked all set to become the first driver to win the championship in his debut season of professional racing, only to be beaten at the last minute and come second by just one point.

Fears

Ailurophobia ·· fear of cats
Belonephobia ································· fear of pins and needles
Coulrophobia ··· fear of clowns
Mycophobia ···································· fear of mushrooms
Triskaidekaphobia ·························· fear of the number 13
Pogonophobia ····································· fear of beards
Pteronophobia ·············· fear of being tickled by feathers
Xanthophobia ··········· fear of the word yellow or yellow things.

Great Snakes

- Nose-horned viper
- Eastern yellowbelly racer
- Rhombic night adder
- Black mamba
- Reticulated python
- Pope's tree viper
- Bushmaster
- Sonoran sidewinder
- Monocled cobra
- Boomslang.

Daredevils

David Blaine
Blaine is a record-breaking magician who once spent 65 hours encased in a solid block of ice.

Alain Robert
Robert is known as the French spiderman for scaling really tall buildings using nothing but his bare hands.

Philippe Petit
Petit is a high-wire artist who walked across a wire strung between the towers of the World Trade Center, a 417m-high (1,368ft) building that used to stand in New York, USA.

Eddie Kidd
Kidd is a motorcycle stuntman who jumped over the Great Wall of China.

Annie Edson Taylor
Taylor went over Niagara Falls in a barrel in 1901, aged 63.

The History Of
The Bicycle

1790 The Célérifère
This had no steering, no pedals, and no chain, but looked quite similar to a modern bike.

1817 The Hobbyhorse
Riders could steer this bike, but bumpy roads made it very uncomfortable to ride.

1860s The Velocipede
This bike was the first to have front wheel pedals. It was popular, even though its wooden (and later metal) tires couldn't cope very well with cobbled streets – which explains its nickname, "the boneshaker."

1870 The Penny Farthing
This inventor realized that the larger a bike's front wheel, the further you could travel with one turn of the pedals. But getting on and off could be a bit tricky, as most penny farthings were over 1.5m (5ft) tall.

1885 The Safety Bicycle
This popular design had gears and a chain – very similar to modern bicycles.

1888 Rubber Tires
When air-filled rubber tires were invented, cycling was no longer a pain in the backside – literally.

Bikes now come in all sorts of styles and sizes, and are made from many materials – from carbon fiber to bamboo.

Deadly Inventions

Some inventors have come up with amazing ideas, only for the worst to happen – their inventions have killed them!

Thomas Midgley Junior was a scientist who invented lead petrol. Later in life he caught the disease polio, and became bedridden. However, it wasn't this that killed him – he actually came up with a complicated system of ropes and pulleys to help him turn over in bed. One day in 1944, he got tangled up in his invention and strangled.

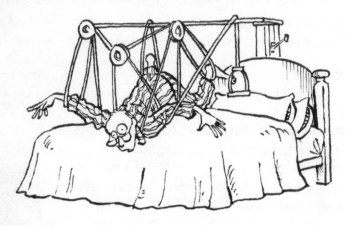

Franz Reichelt was a tailor by day and an inventor in his spare time. He was fascinated by the latest invention – airplanes – and so he put his sewing skills to use, designing an overcoat that acted as a parachute. He tested his new invention using dummies, with varying success. His friends tried to persuade him to reconsider his next test, but Reichelt went ahead and threw himself off the lowest level of the Eiffel Tower … with fatal consequences.

Marie Curie is one of the most famous chemists of all time. She discovered the elements polonium and radium, and developed the Theory of Radioactivity. Unfortunately, she didn't know the dangers of working with radioactive particles, and died from leukaemia (a form of cancer), which was probably caused by her contact with radiation. Her paperwork and research material still exist, but they are so radioactive that they must be stored in protective cases.

Jimi Heselden was a wealthy businessman whose company produced Segways – upright electronic scooters. Although he didn't invent the Segway, it still proved to be Heselden's downfall. While riding a Segway near his estate, he fell off a cliff and drowned in the river below.

Li Si was prime minister for the first emperor of China. He apparently put his intelligence to cruel use when he invented "The Five Pains" – a five-step execution process that, one-by-one, cut off a victim's nose, one of their hands, one of their feet, and their genitals, before finally cutting them in half. Can you guess what happened to him? After the Emperor died, Li Si was found guilty of treason and executed in BC208 – supposedly by his own invention, The Five Pains.

WAIT! I'VE CHANGED HOW THE FIVE PAINS ENDS!

How To Pack

1. Prepare in advance. Make a list and lay out everything you want to take beside your case or backpack.

2. Are you packing for comfort or survival? If you'll be carrying your bag over long distances, be ruthless and remove non-essentials.

3. Ball up your socks and stuff them in your shoes to save space. You don't have to pack pairs of shoes together. Fill gaps with single shoes.

4. Put liquids in a plastic bag in case the bottles leak. You don't want shampoo all over your clothes.

5. Pack in reverse order – put the things you'll need first into your suitcase last, so they're right at the top.

6. Don't fold clothes but roll them instead – it's the most efficient way to fill space and will prevent creases, too.

7. Put anything breakable in the middle of the case and fill the space around it with your rolled-up kit.

8. If you're flying, pack a small "survival" bag to take on board, with essentials for the trip and first day, in case your case gets lost.

How To Make A Million

- Write a number one album and go on non-stop world concert tours

- Discover the cure for baldness

- Write books that become famous films

- Be a brilliant basketball player, golfer, or footballer

- Develop an amazing app

- Live in the United States (where there are more millionaires than anywhere else)

- Create a cure for the common cold

- Work out a simple method of mining the materials found in asteroids, out in space.

BEHOLD MY AMAZING INVENTION, BALD-BE-GONE!

Strange Things People Collect

- Sick bags
- Oil cans
- Belly-button fluff

- Beer mugs
- Rubber ducks
- Key rings

- Toy owls
- Movie cameras
- Toilet seats.

Food Fight!

If you like to throw your food, you should take a trip to the town of Buñol, in Spain, to visit the festival called La Tomatina. Every year on the last Wednesday in August, over 20,000 people descend on the sleepy town to take part in a tomato-throwing fest.

Buildings in the town's main square are covered in plastic sheeting to give some protection from the flying fruit. Everyone gets very messy, but you mustn't forget the golden rule – always squash your tomatoes in your hand before throwing them.

Massive Mountains

The six highest mountains in the world are all in the Himalaya mountain range.

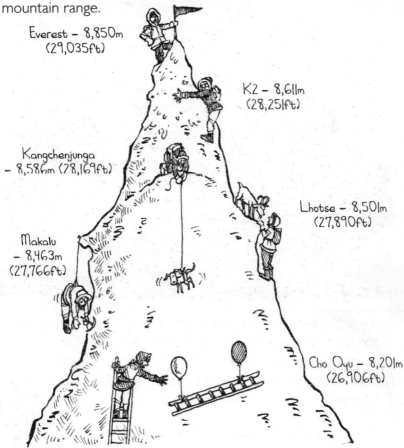

Everest – 8,850m (29,035ft)

K2 – 8,611m (28,251ft)

Kangchenjunga – 8,586m (28,169ft)

Lhotse – 8,501m (27,890ft)

Makalu – 8,463m (27,766ft)

Cho Oyu – 8,201m (26,906ft)

Bad weather and slopes that are tricky to climb mean that mistakes made while mountain-climbing can be fatal. K2 and two smaller but no less brutal mountains – Kangchenjunga and Annapurna 1 – are reckoned to be three of the deadliest mountains on Earth.

Olympics Now And Then

The first Olympic Games were held by the ancient Greeks in 776BC, in Olympia. Now they are held every four years, in countries all around the world. What's changed since the ancient games?

There are 26 sports in the modern Olympics, but when the Olympics first began, there was only a running race. This then expanded to six events – running, wrestling, pentathlon, boxing, chariot-racing, and horse-racing.

Today, the Olympics are broadcast all over the world. When they began, only men and young girls were allowed to watch. If married women were found in the crowd, they were punished.

Men and women from over 200 countries now compete in the games. Back in 776BC, however, only Greek citizens who were free men (not slaves) were allowed to take part. They mainly competed in the nude.

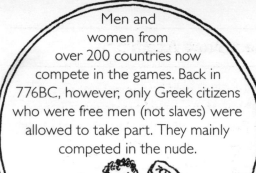

In the modern Olympics, medals are given to the individuals or teams who come first, second, and third in each event. In ancient Greece, only the winner of each event was honored, and given a laurel wreath.

Cheating and fighting are banned from the modern Olympics. In an ancient wrestling event called the *pankration*, competitors could do anything to their opponents – except biting and eye-gouging. But some competitors did both!

The Solar System

Earth isn't the only planet that orbits the Sun. There are eight planets in the Solar System, and each one is a different distance from the Sun. The "Astronomical Unit," or AU, is a

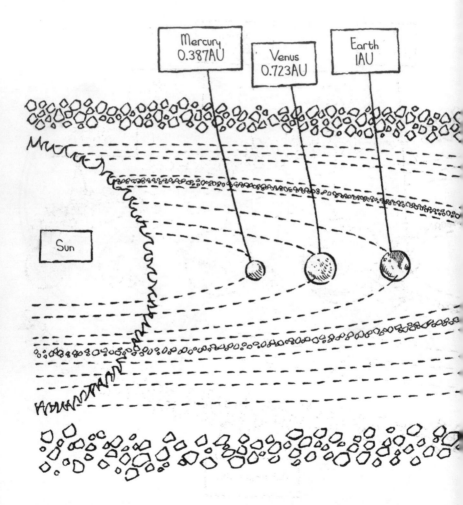

measurement used by space scientists to measure distances in the Solar System. One AU is the distance from the Earth to the Sun – that's 149,597,870.7km (92,955,807.3 miles).

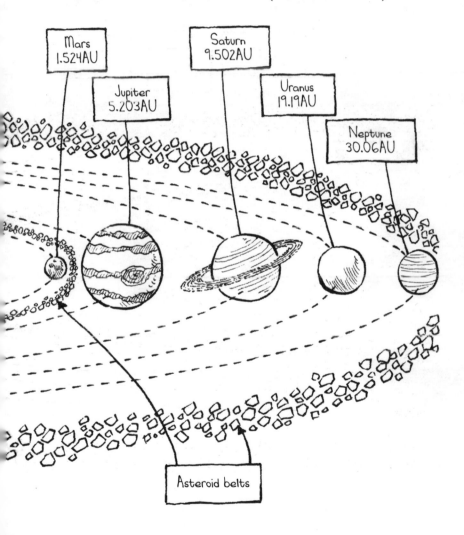

Mars
1.524AU

Jupiter
5.203AU

Saturn
9.502AU

Uranus
19.19AU

Neptune
30.06AU

Asteroid belts

Flying Failures

It took quite a few attempts to create the modern plane – plenty of people tried, and failed, before it finally took off.

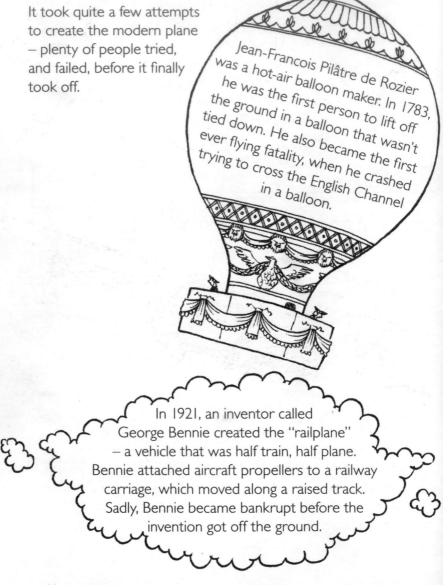

Jean-Francois Pilâtre de Rozier was a hot-air balloon maker. In 1783, he was the first person to lift off the ground in a balloon that wasn't tied down. He also became the first ever flying fatality, when he crashed trying to cross the English Channel in a balloon.

In 1921, an inventor called George Bennie created the "railplane" – a vehicle that was half train, half plane. Bennie attached aircraft propellers to a railway carriage, which moved along a raised track. Sadly, Bennie became bankrupt before the invention got off the ground.

In 1942, Howard Hughes began to design a huge flying boat for use in the Second World War. It was nicknamed the "Spruce Goose" and took its first flight in 1947 – two years after the war ended. The Spruce Goose never flew again.

In 1973, Henry Smolinski created a flying car by strapping the tail and the wings from a small aircraft to a Ford car. Feeling confident, Smolinksi took to the air in his invention. Unfortunately, something went wrong and the car broke away from the airplane parts, with deadly results for the inventor.

Spy Gadgets

Cigarette Case
In 1954, a Soviet (Russian) secret agent revealed that one of his most extraordinary weapons was a deadly cigarette case. Inside was a gun that could shoot poison-tipped bullets.

Paparazzi Pigeons
Before satellites were invented, intelligence agencies used the next best thing – pigeons. These could fly overhead and take photographs with cameras that were strapped to them.

Dart Gun
The head of the American intelligence department, the CIA, unveiled a dart gun in 1975. It was designed to fire a dart that was so tiny it was almost impossible to find, tipped with a poison that wouldn't leave a trace.

Poisoned Umbrella
In 1978, a Bulgarian man called Georgi Markov was walking across a bridge in London when he was jabbed by a passer-by's umbrella. He started feeling ill soon after and died in hospital three days later. Doctors found he had been jabbed in the thigh with a poisoned pellet fired through the tip of the umbrella.

Why Do Two Buses Always Come At Once?

Ever waited for ages for your bus to come, and then found that not one, but two of the buses you want arrive at the same time? Well, there's a reason for that ...

On a busy bus route, buses will leave their garage and start driving along the bus route at regular intervals. But a bus can be slowed down by lots of things — a long line at a bus stop, or a confused customer asking the driver about the destination, or even an accident.

As soon as one bus is delayed, the bus behind it starts to catch up. Because the first bus is running late, the lines will get longer and longer at bus stops further along the route. These passengers will slow down the first bus even more. Eventually, the gap between the two buses will get smaller and smaller until the second one catches up with the first one.

What I Want To Be When I Grow Up

- A candy-taster
- A video-games tester
- A theme-park ride designer
- A surfboard maker
- A stunt double

- A Formula 1 driver
- A luxury-bed tester
- A tropical-island caretaker
- A hot-air balloonist
- A safari guide.

Great Places To ... See All Sorts Of Stars

- Hawaii, USA
- Atacama Desert, Chile
- New Mexico, USA
- Los Angeles, USA
- Kiruna, Sweden
- The Walk of Fame, Hollywood Boulevard, USA. The pavement is filled with stars with the names of lots of different celebrities.

The Country That Lost A Day

It's easy to lose track of time, but have you heard about the country that lost an entire day?

In 2011, the small South Pacific country of Samoa moved across the "International Date Line." This is an imaginary line that runs down the Earth's surface from the North Pole to the South Pole. The date in a country on the west side of the line is one day ahead of any country on the east side of the line.

Samoa chose to move across the line to share the same date as countries that it trades with. So, at midnight on 29th December, Samoa "jumped" from the east side of the line to the west, and skipped forward a day. It missed out 30th December completely. Of course the country didn't actually move – the line was simply redrawn to put the country on the west side.

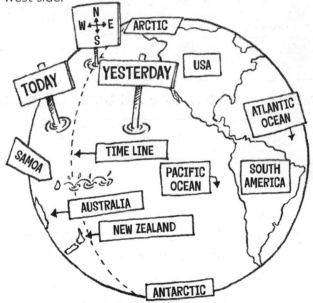

The Man Who Wouldn't Die

Grigori Yefimovich Rasputin was a Russian peasant who became very powerful at the court of the ruler, Tsar Nicholas II, and his wife, Alexandra – but he also made many enemies. Several attempts were made to kill him, but none of them were successful, until in 1916, a group of men finally succeeded. But it wasn't easy! Here is what rumor says happened …

First, Rasputin's murderers fed him poisoned wine and cakes. They waited for the poison to take effect … and waited … and waited. It didn't work!

The killers' next weapon was a pistol. Rasputin was shot and he fell to the floor. The killers left the room to celebrate, but their celebrations were too early. After an hour, one of the men went to check on Rasputin's body. He was horrified when Rasputin sprang to his feet and ran out of the door.

The murderers kept shooting at the retreating Rasputin, who was hit in the back and the head. Surely he was dead now?

Not yet! Rasputin was *still* alive. In desperation, the killers tied him up and wrapped him in a heavy carpet. Then they threw him through a hole in the ice in the nearby Neva River, where he finally drowned.

Hair-Raising Hats

Stovepipe Hat

Montera

Deerstalker

Bowler Hat

Antenna Hat
(to pick up alien signals)

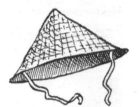

Nón Lá

Fez

Mortar Board

Sombrero

Pirate Hat

Chef's Hat

Knit Cap

How Many Players Are There On A Team?

Soccer 11
Football 11
Field hockey 11
Basketball 5
Baseball 9
Ice hockey 6
Water polo 7
Volleyball 6
Handball 7
Rugby league 13
Rugby union 15
Lacrosse ...... 10 (men's game) 12 (women's game).

How Many Pages Are On The Internet?

The short answer is that no one knows for sure.

The medium answer is that some very clever people have estimated it currently holds about 1,000,000,000,000 pages – give or take the odd million.

The long answer is that no one knows for sure – yet. Sir Tim Berners-Lee (a rather clever guy who's generally thought to be the person who invented the Internet) has set up a group of other experts to try and figure out just how many pages there are.

Rate Your Poop

Scientists at the University of Bristol, UK, have come up with a guide to the most common types of poop – or "stool." It's called "The Stool Form Scale." The type of poop you do depends on how long it has spent in your colon, before it appears in the toilet, and this is affected by your diet and lifestyle.

1. Small, hard, nut-like lumps. These show that you have constipation, and find it hard to poop.

2. Shaped like a lumpy sausage

3. Sausage-shaped but with a cracked surface

4. A smooth, soft sausage shape
A normal poop should look like this.

5. Soft blobs

6. Fluffy, mushy pieces

HMM ... IS THAT A FOUR OR A FIVE?

7. Watery liquid with no solid pieces. This means you have diarrhea, which is unhealthy.

Greek Gods

You've probably heard of Zeus (the leader of the Greek gods) and Poseidon (his brother and ruler of the sea) but the ancient Greeks also worshipped some lesser-known figures.

- The Nine Muses, who offered artistic creativity

- The Winds, spirits who wreaked havoc when they were let loose

- Hades, the god of the Underworld

- Dionysus, god of wine and fruitfulness

- Nike, female goddess of victory

- Hephaestus, god of fire and craftsmen, and the gods' blacksmith

- Hermes, god of messengers, travelers, and tricksters

- Eos, goddess of the dawn

- Persephone, goddess of fertility and nature.

Supercars

Aston Martin	Bugatti	Koenigsegg
Ferrari	Jaguar	Lotus
Porsche	McLaren	Pagani
Lamborghini	Maserati	Mercedes.

How To Spot A Dangerous Shark

Most sharks don't deserve their man-eating reputations. But just in case you spot one in the water, here's a handy guide to spotting the big three you really DO want to avoid.

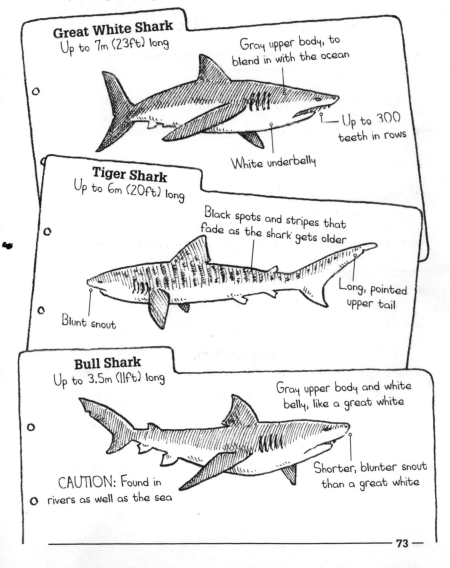

Great White Shark
Up to 7m (23ft) long

Gray upper body, to blend in with the ocean

Up to 300 teeth in rows

White underbelly

Tiger Shark
Up to 6m (20ft) long

Black spots and stripes that fade as the shark gets older

Long, pointed upper tail

Blunt snout

Bull Shark
Up to 3.5m (11ft) long

Gray upper body and white belly, like a great white

Shorter, blunter snout than a great white

CAUTION: Found in rivers as well as the sea

The Deep Blue Sea

The ocean covers 71% of the Earth's surface, but it is hard for humans to explore because of its depth and huge size. Here are some facts to "wet" your appetite.

1,000m (3,280ft)
– the maximum depth sunlight can reach, but below 200m (656ft), only a tiny bit of light penetrates

4,267m (14,000ft)
– the average depth of the ocean

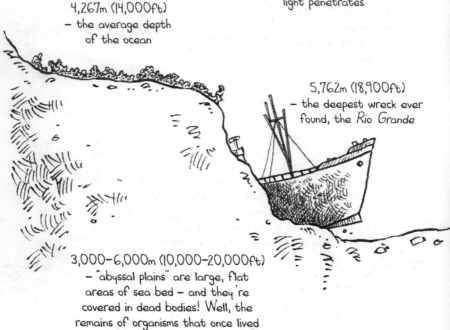

5,762m (18,900ft)
– the deepest wreck ever found, the *Rio Grande*

3,000–6,000m (10,000–20,000ft)
– "abyssal plains" are large, flat areas of sea bed – and they're covered in dead bodies! Well, the remains of organisms that once lived above them, mixed with fine clay.

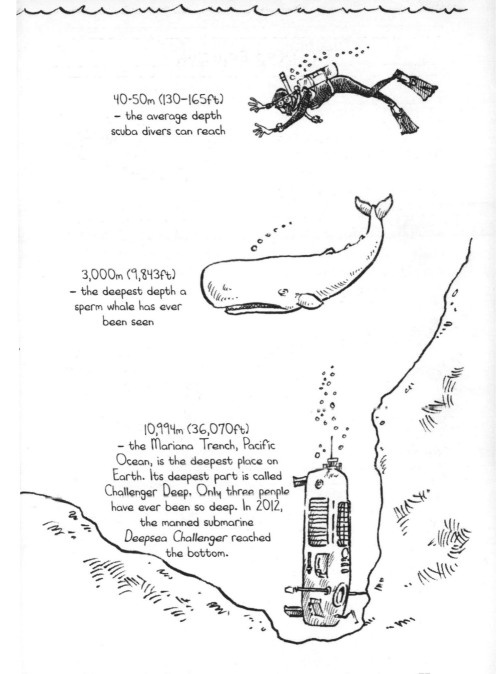

40-50m (130–165ft)
– the average depth
scuba divers can reach

3,000m (9,843ft)
– the deepest depth a
sperm whale has ever
been seen

10,994m (36,070ft)
– the Mariana Trench, Pacific
Ocean, is the deepest place on
Earth. Its deepest part is called
Challenger Deep. Only three people
have ever been so deep. In 2012,
the manned submarine
Deepsea Challenger reached
the bottom.

Disappearing Diseases

Modern medicine is amazing – diseases that once killed millions of people are slowly disappearing or have been wiped out completely.

Whooping Cough

If you hear someone with a horrible, hacking cough, then move away – fast! Whooping cough is highly infectious and very unpleasant, and sufferers make a very strange noise when they cough. It's most dangerous for babies and young children, and a worldwide immunization program is being carried out to reduce the number of people affected by it.

Measles

Being spotty is no joke – especially if you catch measles. This horrible illness spreads easily through coughing or sneezing. It starts as a normal cold but can develop into something far more serious. Measles is rare in most countries, thanks to vaccinations, but the disease still affects people round the world.

Smallpox

Smallpox has been around for years – evidence of it has even been found on the mummified bodies of ancient Egyptians. It causes small swellings on the skin that leave scars called pockmarks. The disease was officially destroyed in 1979 after a vaccine was developed. Now, the only stocks of the smallpox virus that exist are held by the US and Russian governments.

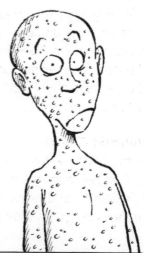

Polio

In the middle of the 20th century, hundreds of thousands of children were struck by the disease polio each year. Severe polio can lead to permanent paralysis of limbs or the muscles that control breathing and, once paralyzed, there is no cure. Vaccines mean that polio has largely vanished, although cases still occur in Afghanistan, India, Pakistan, and Nigeria.

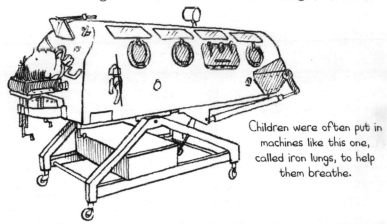

Children were often put in machines like this one, called iron lungs, to help them breathe.

Tuberculosis

Tuberculosis is a horrible disease that affects the lungs. Its telltale symptom is coughing up blood. In the 18th and 19th centuries, the disease was called consumption, and it killed more people in the Western world than any war, natural disaster, or other disease. The invention of antibiotic drugs in the 1940s nearly wiped it out. Today, there are few cases in richer countries, but it's a bigger problem in poorer areas.

Bubonic Plague

In the Middle Ages, the plague wiped out between ¼ and ⅓ of Europe's population. Now it's rare — there are between 1,000 and 3,000 cases each year worldwide. Thanks to modern drugs, it's treatable, but can still sometimes be fatal.

How To Do A Tic Tac In Parkour

Parkour is a sport that makes getting around look cool, by running and jumping over and around obstacles.

One of the most important moves is the tic tac. You run toward the wall, leap up and jump off it, moving forward.

1. Run toward a wall at a 45 degree angle. Keep your eyes on the spot on the wall where you will place your foot.

2. When you are near the wall, jump up and touch it with one foot. Lean your body away from the wall.

3. Make sure the ball of your foot is fully touching the wall so you get a good grip on it. Look forward at the spot you want to land on, and push off the wall with your foot. Don't place your foot too high on the wall. Keep it low and you can push yourself upward.

4. Bring your other knee up and jump outward from the wall. Land on both feet, with your knees bent.

How To Run A Jousting Competition

Although it might look a bit barbaric, jousting was actually a sport played by noblemen in medieval times with a strict set of rules. Here's how to run your own competition.

Before You Start
Get organized by sending out heralds (messengers) to invite challengers from far and wide. Once you've received the names of competitors, rank them in order of ability.
Top Tip – It's a good idea to rank kings or other rich noblemen high up, or you could be up for the chop.

Preparations
Build a stadium to house the large crowds that will be keen to attend. Inside the stadium, you need to build your "tilt yard" – usually a flat, sand-covered enclosure with a wooden barrier to separate riders.

If you're going to take part, make sure you're fitted out in the latest armor. Steel armor cost a lot of money back in the day, so only the rich could afford it – the better the armor, the more powerful you were.
Top Tip – Give your horse some armor to protect its neck and forehead.

Arm Yourself

All that armor weighs a lot, so you'll need to be hoisted on to your horse. Make sure your visor is down, too – although it restricts your vision, it will protect your face from any splinters. Your squire will hand over your lance (a long wooden pole with an arm-guard and blunt spike) and your shield.

Charge!

Wait for the signal from the marshal and the constable, who are in charge of the joust, then dig your spurs into your horse's flanks to start your run.

As you charge, bring your lance up and hold it steady. As the opposing knight hurtles closer, pick the spot you want to hit. The aim is to break his lance, although you can also win a joust by knocking him off his horse.

When your opponent is close enough, thrust with your lance. Keep your shield raised to ward off his blows.

Once you reach the end of your run, your squire should help check out your condition and hand you a new lance if yours has been damaged. Continue charging at each other for the agreed number of passes or until one of you is beaten.

Which Would Win?

- Ant against moth
- Superman against Batman
- Tyrannosaurus Rex against a pack of Velociraptors
- Lara Croft against Max Payne
- Polar bear against lion
- Vampire against werewolf
- Human against zebra
- Wolverine against Spider-Man
- The human race against aliens
- A ninja warrior against a Roman gladiator.

Famous Fictional Fights

- Harry Potter against Lord Voldemort
- Tybalt against Mercutio
- Darth Vader against Obi-Wan Kenobi
- Optimus Prime against Megatron
- Spider-Man against Doctor Octopus
- Gandalf against Saruman.

Mission To Mars?

On 4th November 2011, the thick steel door of the Mars500 spacecraft slowly opened, and six astronauts emerged. Their 520-day mission to Mars had been a complete success … yet their spaceship had never left the ground. What was going on?

In fact, it was all part of an official experiment. The astronauts had volunteered for a pretend mission to Mars. The aim was to see how humans would cope with being in space for such a long time, and the project recreated the sort of conditions that travelers would experience on a real-life mission. These included:

- Being confined within a cramped living space
- Being unable to leave the craft except for a fake Mars walk
- Carrying out scientific experiments on their journey
- A time lag in communications with Earth – it would take up to 25 minutes for a message to be transmitted
- Exercising daily to combat the effects of weightlessness.

Until the technology and the funding are available for a real-life mission to Mars, the six intrepid explorers will remain the closest mankind has got to reaching our distant cousin, the red planet of Mars.

Doggy Data

1. Dogs evolved from a small mammal called a Miacis that looked a bit like a weasel. It lived 60 million years ago.

2. All dogs have 319 bones and 42 adult teeth.

3. Dalmatians aren't born with their spots. Instead, they are born white and their spots appear a few days later.

4. Dogs' nose prints are as individual as humans' fingerprints, and so they can be used to identify them.

5. Dogs sweat through the pads of their feet.

6. Not all dogs bark – a breed called the basenji makes a yodeling, howling sound when it is happy.

Know Your Roman Numerals

I (unus) = 1
V (quinque) = 5
X (decem) = 10
L (quinquaginta) = 50
C (centum) = 100
D (quingenti) = 500
M (mille) = 1,000

Bigger numbers are shown by adding a line on top of a numeral, which multiplies it by 1,000. For example:

$\overline{V}$ = 5,000
$\overline{L}$ = 50,000
$\overline{C}$ = 100,000.

Pick A Pooch

Boxer	Poodle	Weimaraner
Dalmation	Papillon	Chow Chow
Siberian Husky	Doberman	Corgi
Rottweiler	Pug	Border Collie
Beagle	Pointer	Great Dane
Alaskan Malamute	German Shepherd	Bulldog.

Great Places To ...
See Extreme Horse-Riding Skills

- With gauchos (real-life cowboys) on a ranch in Argentina
- At a polo match in Europe, Argentina, or the USA
- During the Calgary stampede in Canada
- In Central Asia during games of "*Buzkashi*," where teams on horseback score points by throwing a goat's carcass into a special area.

How To Avoid Being Eaten

Some animals have come up with rather creative ways to avoid becoming lunch.

Horned Lizards squirt blood up to 1m (3ft) from their eyes, which confuses predators, and is poisonous to dogs, wolves, and coyotes.

Spanish Ribbed Newts protect themselves by pushing their ribs through their skin to form a row of sharp, pointed arrows. Each arrow is tipped with poison from the newt's skin.

Sea Cucumbers are animals that live underwater and look like warty cucumbers. They can expel their internal organs through their behinds to distract predators, and then grow new ones.

Squid squirt out clouds of black ink when they are threatened, which hide them while they make their getaway.

Bombardier Beetles eject a boiling hot jet of foul-smelling liquid with an explosive pop from their bottoms when they are attacked. The noise, heat, and stink are enough to put any predator off.

Violent Volcanoes

One way to measure the strength of volcanic eruptions is to use a scale called the Volcanic Explosivity Index. This has a scale that ranges from 0 to 8, from small and quiet eruptions, through cataclysmic, supercolossal, and finally, at the top of the scale, megacolossal.

Megacolossal eruptions only happen every 10,000 years, but when they do, you know about it. Megacolossal eruptions include the one at Lake Toba, in Sumatra, which happened more than 70,000 years ago and carved out the world's largest volcanic crater.

Great Places To ...
Get Close To A Live Volcano

- Mount Etna, Italy
- Eyjafjallajokull, Iceland
- Cerro Arenal, Costa Rica
- Kilauea, Hawaii
- Pacaya, Guatemala.

Email Events

1971 – The first email message was sent by a computer programmer called Ray Tomlinson. He was working on an early version of the Internet. Unfortunately, Tomlinson can't remember what he wrote, but he thinks it was probably something rather dull, like "QWERTYIOP," "testing 123," or information about how to use the @ sign.

1976 – Queen Elizabeth II of England became the first head of state to send an email.

1982 – This was a big year for emails. It was the year that the term email (short for electronic mail) began to be used, and it was also probably the first time that a computer professor in the US created a smiley face emoticon :).

1991 – The first email was sent from space.

1998 – The word SPAM entered dictionaries. This word for junk email is thought to have come from a comic sketch by British comedy group Monty Python. The sketch shows two characters choosing items from a menu filled with spam products, before a group of Vikings start chanting "SPAM."

The Schmidt Pain Index

Justin O. Schmidt is a scientist who studies insects, and during his career he has been stung by lots of them. So he came up with the "Schmidt Pain Index," a scale that describes the pain he and his workmates felt when they were stung. The best thing about the scale is the hilarious way in which Schmidt describes the pain he felt. Here are some highlights.

Bald Faced Hornet
"Rich, hearty, slightly crunchy. Similar to getting your hand mashed in a revolving door."

Bullhorn Acacia Ant
"A rare, piercing, elevated sort of pain; someone has fired a staple into your cheek."

Harvester Ant
"Bold and unrelenting — somebody is using a power drill to excavate your ingrown toenail."

Bullet Ant
"Pure, intense, brilliant pain, like walking over flaming charcoal with a three-inch nail embedded in your heel."

Great Places To ...
Take Part In A Street Carnival

- Rio de Janeiro, Brazil
- New Orleans, USA
- Cologne, Germany
- Aalborg, Denmark
- Venice, Italy.

Dream Den

If you were given complete control and an unlimited budget to design your own crib, what would you do? Here are some suggestions to start you thinking about your room.

- A parent alert to let you know when they're approaching

- An automatic outfit selector – to take the stress out of picking the perfect clothes

- A massive screen for video games and TV

- An instant makeover button that makes the floor rotate to reveal a tidy room

- A vending machine stuffed with goodies to snack on

- An instant pizza button, linked to your favorite pizza restaurant

- An ejector flume that shoots you straight into town, school, or any other destination of your choice

- A chill zone with plenty of space to chill out on bean bags and reclining chairs

- An intruder alarm to protect your dream den.

Foul Feet

Your feet can suffer all sorts of foul fungi and painful growths.

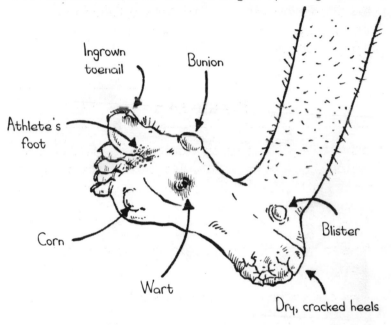

Ingrown toenail

Bunion

Athlete's foot

Corn

Wart

Blister

Dry, cracked heels

Did You(Tube) Know?

The first video ever posted on YouTube was 19 seconds long and shot in San Diego Zoo. The clip was uploaded on 23rd April 2005 and showed co-founder Jawed Karim with some elephants. If you go to the site, you can still watch it.

According to YouTube, about 48 hours of video content are uploaded every minute. That's almost eight years worth of watching added every day!

Horrible Jobs From History

Tooth Donor

In the 18th century you could make money out of your mouth by giving your teeth to people whose own chompers had rotted. But you wouldn't have any painkillers while they pulled yours out!

A Fuller's Apprentice

"Fullers" worked with cloth in medieval times. As an apprentice, you would use your feet to tread a mixture of ground clay and two-week-old urine into wool. You'd need fancy footwork and a not-so-sensitive nose.

Food Taster

Throughout history, powerful rulers have had enemies. Food-tasters were employed to eat a little of the royal food and wine before the king or queen did. That way, it would be the food-taster who died if there was anything sketchy about the dinner. It is said Emperor Hirohito of Japan had a food-taster at his palace to check his food in the early 20th century.

Chimney Sweep

Here's another vile Victorian job. Boys as young as four years old would climb up inside sooty chimneys and sweep them clean. They would get completely filthy, and develop red eyes and grazed skin with infected sores. After a while, they would often develop hacking coughs from all the soot they breathed in – but don't worry, they could retire at 15, when they got too big for the job.

Gong (Toilet) Scourer

Before flushing toilets and modern sewers were invented, human waste ended up in large pools called cesspits – and somebody had to clean them out. You'd have needed a strong stomach, and to watch your step in the slippery conditions.

Great Places To ... Photograph The Big Five

The "big five" are animals that are difficult to spot on safari. They are lions, rhinos, elephants, cape buffalos, and leopards. Here's where you can catch a glimpse ...

- Kruger Park, South Africa
- Masai Mara National Reserve, Kenya
- Serengeti, Tanzania
- Chobe National Park, Botswana
- Etosha National Park, Namibia.

Cool Scooter Tricks

Bunny Hop
With both feet on the deck of the scooter, bend your knees, and then jump up. Keep the deck tightly against your feet by pulling up on the handlebars when you jump. Land with your deck straight, or you might go flying.

Wheelie
Move both feet to the back of your deck. Pull up on your handlebars, and reduce the weight on your front foot. Keep your back foot on the deck. Try to lift the front wheel, but keep the back wheel on the ground.

Jayhop
This is a cross between a wheelie and a bunny hop. First do a wheelie, and while your front wheel is in the air, try a bunny hop. Both wheels should leave the ground, but the front wheel should be higher than the back wheel.

Stall

This trick takes a jayhop to the next level. Find a raised surface, like a bench, rail, or curb. Jayhop on to it, balance for as long as you can, and then jayhop back on to the ground. It doesn't count if you just fall off!

Tail Whip

First do a bunny hop. While your deck is in the air, kick it with your back foot so it swings around in a circle (360°). When your deck comes back around and is beneath your feet again, push your feet down hard on the deck to land.

Front Wheelie

This is like a backward wheelie, where you lift up your back wheel. Place your feet at the front of the deck. Push forward on your bars while pushing down on your front foot, so that the back of your deck lifts up. Be careful not to land on your face!

Bloody Battles

Here are some tragic conflicts from history where the casualties really piled up.

Battle Of Gettysburg

When: 1863, in the American Civil War
Between: Different states in America, divided into Union and Confederate forces
Casualties: Around 50,000
Victor: The Union forces

Battle Of Cannae

When: 216BC
Between: The Romans and the Carthaginians
Casualties: Around 60,000
Victor: Carthage

Battle Of Red Cliff

When: 208 or 209AD, China
Between: Two generals, Sun Quan, who controlled southern China, and Cao Cao, who controlled northern China
Casualties: Around 100,000
Victor: Sun Quan

First Battle Of The Somme

When: 1916, during the First World War
Between: Combined British and French forces, and the German army
Casualties: Around 1¼ million
Victor: Neither. The war continued for two more years.

Battle Of Stalingrad

When: 1942–3, during the Second World War
Between: Russian forces and the German army
Casualties: Up to 2 million
Victor: Russia.

Great Places To ... Scuba Dive

- The Great Barrier Reef, Australia
- The Florida Keys, USA
- The Cayman Islands
- The Bahamas
- The Red Sea.

Paper Money

The first recorded use of paper money was in China, more than 1,000 years ago.

The most expensive bill ever is a rare American $1,000 bill that sold for over $2,000,000 in December 2006.

In 1946 the Hungarian National Bank produced the 100 quintillion pengö bill – if you wrote that out in figures it would have 20 zeros! To make it easier for people to use the bill, the number was written out in words on the bill.

In 1917 the Ministry of Finance of Romania issued the smallest ever national bill, the 10-bani bill. The area that was printed upon measured 2.75 × 3.8cm (1.08 × 1.49in). This is roughly $\frac{1}{10}$ the size of a dollar bill.

Toilet Trivia From The Animal World

The study of poop is called scatology. Here are some fecal (poop-related) facts to enjoy.

- A fossilized poop is called a coprolite. The largest dinosaur coprolite ever found is 44cm (17in) long and weighs over 7kg (15lb). Scientists think it came from a Tyrannosaurus Rex.

- Birds, amphibians, and reptiles don't have separate openings for pee and poop – they only have one opening called a cloaca, and their waste products come out together, as a paste.

- Rabbits are prolific poopers – they can produce 500 pellets of poop a day. They also sometimes produce a special kind of poop called a cecotrope, which they eat. This contains vitamins that help them digest their food.

- There is a rare and expensive kind of coffee called Kopi Luwak. Why is it so special? Because the Indonesian civet cat eats the coffee beans and then poops them out, before they are turned into coffee.

- Because camels live in the desert, they don't want to waste water. Their droppings are so dry when they are pooped out that you could strike a match and burn them immediately.

- Wolverines are a kind of wild cat that poop all over their prey once they've had a meal from it. This stops other animals eating the leftovers, but it can't taste very good when they go back for seconds!

Red Hot Chilli Peppers

Named after its creator, Walter Scoville, the Scoville Scale measures the strength (or heat) of chilli peppers in Scoville Heat Units (SHU). Here are the coolest and hottest chillis around.

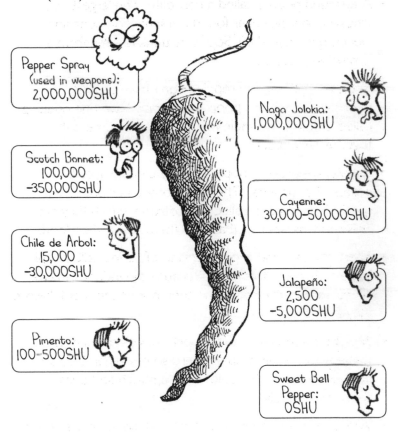

Pepper Spray (used in weapons): 2,000,000SHU

Naga Jolokia: 1,000,000SHU

Scotch Bonnet: 100,000 -350,000SHU

Cayenne: 30,000-50,000SHU

Chile de Arbol: 15,000 -30,000SHU

Jalapeño: 2,500 -5,000SHU

Pimento: 100-500SHU

Sweet Bell Pepper: 0SHU

If you eat a chilli but can't handle the heat, don't gulp water. Instead, drink a milk-based product. If the chilli really burns, try swilling your mouth out with vegetable oil and then spitting it out.

Uninventive Names

A few famous inventors have given their names to their world-famous discoveries.

Jim Bowie ·· hunting knife
Laslo Biro ··· pen
Erno Rubix ··· Rubix cube
James Dyson ·· vacuum cleaner
King Gillette ··· safety razor
Rudolf Diesel ··· vehicle engine
Robert Moog ·· synthesizer
Louis Braille ··················· writing system for the blind
Michael Kalashnikov ································· rifle
Ray Dolby ······················· noise reduction system.

Brilliant Beetles

If you hate creepy-crawlies, look away now!

- Biscuit beetles
- Bark-gnawing beetles
- Goliath beetles
- Leaf-rolling beetles
- Monkey beetles

- Rhinoceros beetles
- Stag beetles
- Tiger beetles
- Whirligig beetles.

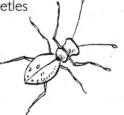

Why Do You Dream?

Dreams help your brain store memories. While you sleep, your brain reorganizes your memories to make sure you remember the most important things. It is a little bit like saving work that you do on the computer in a special place. That's why sleeping after revising for a test is really important – it helps strengthen your memory and helps you store the information you have learned.

Dreams help people make sense of their own lives and help with problem solving – that's why some people say "sleep on it" before making a difficult decision.

Vivid dreams mostly occur during a certain stage or cycle of sleep known as REM (Rapid Eye Movement) sleep.

Some people believe that you can actually control dreams and choose what you would like to dream about. This process is known as "lucid dreaming." Imagine it ... you could have your favorite dream every night!

Seven Smart Animals

Some animals are extremely brainy beasts — here are seven of the most cunning creatures.

Pigs enjoy playing soccer, and listening to music — not necessarily at the same time. They also have very long memories. One scientist taught some pigs to jump over dumbbells and fetch Frisbees. Three years later, the pigs could still remember what they had been taught.

Rats have a bad reputation for being dirty pests, but they're actually rather clever. They have been known to find shortcuts, loopholes, and escape routes in the laboratory experiments designed by top scientists.

Dolphins talk to each other using a complex language, although humans have only just begun to unravel it. Dolphins also use tools in their natural environment. The clever mammals shake large conch shells with their beaks. This drains the water out of the shells and means that any fish that are hiding inside fall into the dolphins' mouths as lunch.

Crows living in cities are known to gather nuts from trees, and then place them in the street for passing cars to drive over, cracking open the shells.

Pigeons are far from being birdbrains. They can recognize hundreds of images even after several years have passed. They can also identify themselves in mirrors.

Chimpanzees can make and use tools, hunt as teams, and are capable of advanced problem-solving. They are also able to learn sign language to communicate with humans and can remember the name sign for individuals they have not seen for several years.

Octopuses have great memories. Once an octopus has learned how to do something, it doesn't forget. Octopuses can also solve puzzles and navigate through mazes. Octi the octopus, kept by a family in a pool in New Zealand, worked out how to open a bottle containing live crabs. They're not just clever, they're also flexible. If an octopus finds itself in a tight spot facing a predator, it can escape by squeezing through a hole no bigger than one of its eyes!

How To Tell If Your Neighbor is ...

... An Alien

- Strange noises and lights seen coming from their home
- Advanced knowledge of astronomy
- Vague about their home town
- A rather slimey handshake
- Tentacles poke out from beneath their clothes.

.... A Vampire

- Allergic to garlic
- Wears black
- Never seen in daylight
- Sleeps in a coffin
- Surprising level of knowledge about events that happened hundreds of years ago.

... A Werewolf
- Explosive rage
- Ability to howl at the moon
- Never around on a night of a full moon
- Looks tired after a full moon has waned
- Huge, hairy ears and eyebrows.

... A Superhero
- Often vanishes from parties or meetings without warning
- Extremely fit and muscly
- Loves costumes
- Not many friends, due to their habit of leaving parties so suddenly.

A Staring Contest

Don't try to beat a goldfish in a staring competition – you can't. Goldfish don't have eyelids, so they can't blink.

Be A Record Breaker

Why not make a name for yourself by becoming a record breaker? Here are some records you might want to target.

- Ollies on a skateboard
- Fastest mile on a space hopper
- Longest fingernails
- Longest ride on a theme-park attraction
- Fastest mile on a pogo stick while juggling
- Most bunny hops on a bicycle
- Most high-fives in a minute
- Fastest motorized sofa
- Longest tongue
- Most socks worn on one foot.

Sensible Superpowers

Superman can fly and Spider-Man can shoot webs, but you might prefer to have superpowers that are more useful in day-to-day situations.

Super-Charged Sleeping
Get eight hours of sleep in eight minutes.

Power Up
Zap your mobile, laptop, or electric car battery to full power when it's out of juice.

Speed Machine
Write as fast as you think, so you can whizz through your homework at top speed.

Ball Control
Control the ball with your mind to help your team win every game.

Job Done
Make your bed, tidy your room, or unload the dishwasher – instantly.

Green For Go
Point your finger at those annoying red traffic lights to change them to green.

Weather Man
Make the sun shine whenever you want.

Magic Mute
Make your terrifying teacher speechless.

Super Stretch
See around corners, look over walls, and turn the lights on or off without getting up.

Liquidation
Magically refill a cup or glass so it's never empty.

Virtual Skill Set
Be as athletic or strong in real life as you are in video games.

True Or False Teeth

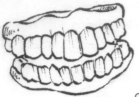

Did you think that putting effort into getting a great set of chompers is just a 21st-century habit? Think again.

False teeth have been found that date back to around 700BC. Historians think they were invented by a civilization of people called Etruscans who carved them out of wood or animal teeth.

The oldest complete set of dentures that has been discovered was carved out of cherry wood in 14th-century Japan. They were made for an important priestess.

In the Middle Ages and beyond, Europeans would take teeth from corpses or children to replace their own rotten chompers. By this time, rich people would also have false teeth fitted that were made of gold, silver, mother-of-pearl, or ivory.

In 1785, an American dentist, Dr. John Greenwood, introduced porcelain dentures. Unfortunately, his invention had a few teething problems (sorry!) – they didn't fit well, were an odd color, and often smashed.

Musical Genres

Classical
Country
Jazz
Blues
Reggae
R 'n' B
Rock
Indie
Dance
Electronica
Pop
Folk
Easy Listening
Grunge
Punk

Drum and Bass
Dubstep
Garage
House
Techno

Hip-Hop
Rap
Ska

Motown
Disco
Death Metal.

That's A Mouthful

What counts as a full set of chompers in the animal world?

Elephant ·· 24
Dog ·· 42
Cat ·· 30
Great white shark ···························· up to 300 at a time
Adult human ··· 32
Tyrannosaurus Rex ·· 60
Giraffe ·· 32
Crocodile ·· up to 72
Narwhal ·········· 2 (one tooth grows as the long tusk)
Bottlenose dolphin ··· 100.

How To Juggle

1. Get the right equipment – juggling balls are best, or soft, squishy, mini beanbags. You can always choose apples or other fruit, but they're harder to catch. Save them for when you're a pro.

2. Start with one ball and throw it gently from one hand to the other. Practice letting the ball go up to about the level of your nose and then down into the other hand.

Swap your throwing and catching hands so you're equally comfortable throwing the ball with either one.

3. Now add a second ball and hold it in your catching hand. Throw the first ball in an arc, as you've practiced. When it reaches the peak of its arc, throw the ball in the other hand. You should then be able to catch one, then the other ball.

4. Keep going until you are comfortable with throwing and catching both balls – keep focusing on the arc motion. Once you've mastered these steps, you're ready to add ball number three.

5. Take a deep breath and relax. Hold two balls (A and C) in your right hand and one (B) in your left one. Swap if you're left-handed.

6. Repeat step **3**, as you've been practicing, and throw ball A and then ball B.

C – throw when you catch A.

About to catch B

A – just caught

7. As soon as you catch ball A in your left hand, throw ball C. Straight afterward, catch ball B in your right hand, and then catch ball C in your left.

Congratulations – you've completed your first juggle.

8. Repeat steps **5** to **7**, but don't stop – keep throwing the balls in the same order. Continue practicing and you'll find you soon become more confident and able to juggle faster.

Cloud Spotting

Can you look up and name the clouds in the sky? Here's a quick guide.

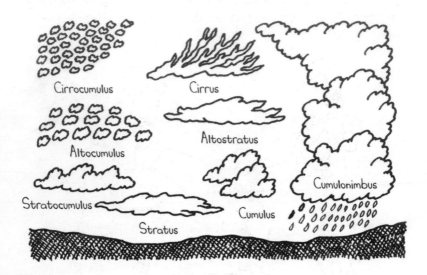

Clouds are divided into three groups – depending on their height above the ground.

- The highest clouds are cirrus and cirrocumulus. They are small and wispy.

- The clouds in the middle are altocumulus, which are small and fleecy, and altostratus, which are rounded.

- The lowest clouds are stratocumulus, stratus, and cumulus. They are usually gray and bring rain.

A cloud that extends through each level is called a cumulonimbus.

Shake It

It's generally thought that men started shaking hands in medieval times as a way of showing strangers that they weren't carrying any weapons, and were meeting for peaceful reasons. As women weren't usually armed, they didn't shake hands at all.

Precious Metals

Here's our pick of the world's most precious metals.

Indium   Palladium   Ruthenium
Silver   Osmium   Gold
Rhenium   Iridium   Platinum.

How To Boost Your Pocket Money

When you find yourself a little short on funds, here are some sure-fire ways to top up your wallet.

1. Do a little IT support at home. Upgrade the software on your folks' computers, tidy up their desktops, and organize all the photos into albums. Ask first, of course!

2. Start a pet-sitting service. If you can't do pet-sitting, why not offer your services as a dog walker?

3. Wash the windows. Make them so shiny and streak-free that people can't even see that they're there.

4. Sell some spare stuff. Offer to help your folks get rid of all their spare stuff online for a small percentage of the profit.

5. Get into puncture repairs or be a bike mechanic. Help your family and neighbors to keep their bikes in tip-top condition.

Slips Of The Tongue

Famous words which may have later been regretted …

"They couldn't hit an elephant at this distance."
General John Sedgwick, just before he was fatally shot in the
American Civil War.

"It will be gone by June."
Variety magazine in 1955, talking about rock 'n' roll.

"This 'telephone' … is of no value to us."
Telegram company Western Union's response to Bell's rather
useful invention.

"It will be years – not in my time – before a woman will
become prime minister."
Margaret Thatcher, just nine years before she became – yes,
you've guessed it – Britain's first female prime minister.

Big Cats

There are lots of large furry felines, but did you know that
the term "big cats" only applies to leopards, lions, tigers, and
jaguars? These are the only four cats that can roar.

Feeling Blue?

In the 1960s, a young doctor working in a remote part of Kentucky, USA, was amazed when two people walked into his medical center. They looked nothing like anyone else he had ever seen – because their faces and fingers were a deep blue color.

After asking them a number of questions and looking up their medical records, the doctor discovered that there were more "blue" people, and they were all related. They were all descended from one man, called Martin Fugate, and carried a gene that gave them this remarkable appearance.

Often, blue skin is a sign that someone is suffering from a heart attack or being suffocated. But these people were in perfect health, and the blue-skinned people normally lived longer than other, non-blue people!

After a few months consulting with other experts, the doctor injected each blue-skinned person with a substance called methylene blue. This is a blue liquid normally used to treat the disease malaria. Within days, it corrected the genetic imbalance and the blue people's skin slowly returned to a more normal pink color.

As the people with blue skin married people without the "blue" gene, fewer babies with the condition were born, and it's believed that the blue-skinned people of Kentucky have almost completely died out now.

Chinese Animal Years

What animal are you? Find the year you were born.

Shades Of Blue

- Azure
- Cobalt
- Electric
- Sky
- Teal

- Prussian
- Steel
- Royal
- Cyan
- Sapphire

- Turquoise
- Cornflower
- Powder
- Iris
- Egyptian.

Time For Tea?

Legend has it that tea was first drunk in China as early as 2700 BC. It was described as "the froth of liquid jade." Until the 3rd century AD, tea was usually drunk as a medicinal remedy. During the 6th century AD, it began to be enjoyed as a social drink.

As trade between the East and West developed in the 16th century, tea-drinking was introduced to wealthy people in Europe. The success of tea was partly based on the strategy of using it to fill empty cargo ships on the return leg of their trading trips to China. As trade increased in the 18th century, tea prices dropped, which led to a huge growth in its popularity among ordinary people.

At the start of the 20th century, a New York tea merchant called Thomas Sullivan began sending tea samples to customers in white silk bags. His invention of tea bags meant it was even easier to drink tea – making it even more popular.

Today, tea is enjoyed in over 40 countries worldwide.

Naming Nebulae

"Nebulae" are giant clouds of gas or dust out in space. Some of them have been given great names.

- Bug Nebula
- Stingray Nebula
- Cat's Eye Nebula
- Hourglass Nebula
- Ant Nebula
- Boomerang Nebula
- Eskimo Nebula

- Red Rectangle Nebula
- Rotten Egg Nebula
- Crab Nebula
- Horsehead Nebula
- Gum Nebula
- Witch Head Nebula
- Wizard Nebula.

Not all hamburgers are tasty – Gomez's Hamburger is a nebula that is 900 light-years away from Earth. The "buns" are made from reflective dust, and the "burger" is made of dark dust.

I DIDN'T THINK IT WAS A *REAL* HAMBURGER!

Knockout Nicknames

You might be the meanest wrestler in the world, but without a memorable name your career's never going to get off the ground. Here are some wrestlers with brilliant names.

- Stone Cold Steve Austin – The Texas Rattlesnake

- John Cena – The Doctor of Thuganomics

- Hulk Hogan – The Immortal

- Chris Benoit – The Rabid Wolverine

- Randy Orton – The Legend Killer

- Christian – Captain Charisma

- Kane – The Big Red Machine

- Randy Savage – Macho Man

- Umaga – The Samoan Bulldozer

- MVP – Half Man, Half Amazing.

Kiss Or Shake Hands?

Why is kissing more hygienic than shaking hands? It's down to two things: people generally aren't very good about washing their hands, and there's more skin-to-skin contact when you shake hands than kiss, so there's more chance of germs spreading.

Pencil Power

Although graphite was first used to write with by the Aztecs, the modern pencil was invented by a scientist working for French general Napoleon Bonaparte's army in 1795.

The magic ingredient in every pencil is graphite – a form of pure carbon. As one of the softest solids known to mankind, it is able to stay together while also leaving a black mark when pressed against paper. Strangely, another form of carbon is diamond – one of the hardest solids on the planet.

Hunger Games Districts

District 1 – Jewels and luxury items
District 2 – Masonry and military equipment
District 3 – Technology and electronics
District 4 – Fishing
District 5 – Scientific research
District 6 – Medical
District 7 – Wood, timber, and paper
District 8 – Textiles
District 9 – Food processing and grain
District 10 – Livestock (farm animals)
District 11 – Farming
District 12 – Coal mining
District 13 (thought to have been destroyed) – Graphite mining (and secret nuclear development).

Shiny New Species

The world's a pretty big place, and new species of animals are being discovered all the time. Here are some amazing animals that have been found around the world.

Sneezing Monkey

The sneezing monkey was discovered in Myanmar. It looks a little like Lord Voldemort, with a snubbed nose, and it sneezes when it rains. Achoo!

Flasher Wrasse

The male flasher wrasse is an Indonesian fish that can flash electric blue patterns on its skin. It creates this amazing light show in the afternoons to attract females.

Dracula Minnow
This small fish from Myanmar has two tiny fangs shaped like a vampire's that it uses to fight other males.

Sazima's Tarantula
Found in Brazil, this big hairy spider is a striking navy blue.

Lost World Tree Mouse
The lost world tree mouse lives in an aerial kingdom, barely touching the ground. It lives in the jungles of Indonesia, and travels using tree branches and vines as roads.

E.T. Salamander
The E.T. salamander was discovered in Ecuador. It's a lizard that doesn't have lungs, but breathes through its skin instead. It was named becuase it looks like the friendly alien from a film called *E.T. – The Extra Terrestrial.*

Spike-Nosed Tree Frog
This frog is also known as the "Pinocchio frog" because of its long nose, which points upward when it makes a noise, but deflates back down afterward.

How To Stage Fight

The key to a great stage fight is to agree your movements in advance and practice them slowly before gradually building up your speed. You should never go too fast – stage fights usually happen at about 80% of the speed of a real-life fight. To avoid accidents when stage fighting, always take great care.

The Punch

1. Decide who is going to throw the punch, who is going to be hit and whether it will be a body or chin blow. Make sure your opponent knows what to expect.

2. Get into position – stand facing each other an arm's length away. Measure this by stretching out your arms and putting your hands on each other's shoulders. Make sure you are both side-on to your audience.

3. Imagine a frame around the recipient's head – you should aim to hit one of the corners of this frame and then continue with your follow-through, past his or her head. Don't stop your punch in front of their head.

4. Count to three, then throw the punch.

5. The person who throws the punch with one hand should slap the top part of their chest with their other hand to make a realistic impact sound. Timing's important here – the chest thump should coincide with the punch "landing."

6. The person who is "hit" should then react by throwing their head backward.

7. Practice the punch until all the elements come together. Once you can throw and receive fake punches, think about putting together a combination of two or three.

BAM! POW! BIFF!

The Slap

1. Get prepared and into position, as above. Start counting from one to three. On the count of two, the person who is being "slapped" should raise their hand to the side of their face that the audience can't see.

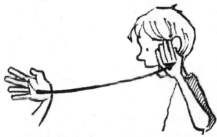

2. On three, the person administering the slap then steps forward and aims their slap on the hand of the other person.

3. The person being slapped should then react by crying in pain or surprise.

Once you've mastered the moves above, put them together in any combination to create an even longer fight scene.

Killer Queens

Here are some queens who liked nothing more than being ruthless.

Ranavalona, Queen Of Madagascar (1788–1861)
After her husband King Radama died, Ranavalona declared herself queen and started her reign of terror by:

- Killing any rivals who didn't accept her as ruler.

- Taking part in a secret accession ceremony in which her body was sprinkled with bull's blood.

- Driving Europeans off the island. The Queen's men cut the heads off their victims and stuck them on spears on the beach as a warning to her opponents.

- Torturing, beheading, poisoning, or boiling in water anyone caught practicing Christianity.

- Selling her own people off as slaves. By the end of her reign, it's thought that the population of the island had been reduced from 5 million people down to 2.5 million!

Empress Wu Zetian (624–705)

Wu Zetian was the only female emperor in Chinese history. As she rose to power she got rid of her rivals by:

- Strangling her own daughter, then framing her rivals for the murder.

- Cutting off enemies' hands and feet then throwing them into wells to drown.

- Creating a secret police force to spy on opponents. Needless to say, anyone who was seen as a threat was quickly dealt with.

Fredegund, Queen Of Neustrua (?–597)

If the account by historian Gregory of Tours is believed, Fredegund, a Frankish queen, carried out a long list of murderous acts, including:

- Attempting to murder her daughter, Rigunth, by closing the lid of a chest on her throat.

- Having her stepson and his girlfriend stabbed to death for making "unforgiveable remarks" about her.

- Hosting a banquet that ended with three guests having their heads chopped off for quarrelling.

Goodbye

German – *Auf wiedersehen*
("Owf vee-der-zayn")

French – *Au revoir*
("Oh rev-wah")

Spanish – *Adiós* ("Ad-ee-os")

Dutch – *Tot ziens*
("Toht zeens")

Polish – *Do widzenia*
("Do vid-zen-ya")

Norwegian – *Ha det bra*
("Ha day bra")

Swedish – *Hej då*
("Hay daw").